AN EYE-WITNESS ACCOUNT OF WHITE SLAVERY UNDER THE MOORS

FRANCIS BROOKS

OSTARA PUBLICATIONS

Barbarian Cruelty
By Francis Brooks
Being A True History of the Distressed Condition of the Christian Captives under the Tyranny of *Mully Ishmael* Emperor of *Morocco*, and King of *Fez* and *Macqueness* in *Barbary*.
In which is likewise given a particular Account of his late Wars with the *Algerines*. The manner of his Pirates taking the Christians and Others. His breach of Faith with Christian Princes.
A Description of his Castles and Guards, and the Places where he keeps his Women, his Slaves and Negroes. With a particular Relation of the dangerous Escape of the Author, and two English Men more from thence, after a miserable Slavery of ten Years.
By Francis Brooks. London: 1693.
Printed for J. Salusbury at the Rising-Sun in *Cornhil*, and H. Markman at the King's Arms in the *Poultry*. MDCXCIII.

This edition
Ostara Publications 2013

www.ostarapublications.com

ISBN 9781684546121

Contents

Europe Under Attack—Introduction to the 2013 Edition

It is a simple fact of the anti-white establishment that the Trans-Atlantic slave trade is known to all, but knowledge of the Muslim slave-trade in Europeans is deliberately suppressed.

Europeans are continually "blamed" for African slavery (even though only a tiny minority were ever involved in it, and it was Europeans who brought it to an end), but no-one ever dares "blame" the Muslim world for their slave trade in Africans and Europeans, which lasted for centuries longer than the Atlantic slave trade.

It was during the 1600s that Barbary corsairs—pirates from the Barbary Coast of North Africa (today Algeria, Libya and Morocco)—were at their most active and terrible. With the full support of the Moorish rulers of North Africa, these Muslim slavers raided southern Europe, the Atlantic European coast, Britain and Ireland almost at will.

Over one million Europeans were captured and enslaved in these raids, carried out upon ships and land settlements alike. British Admiralty records show that 466 vessels were seized off the coast of England between 1609 and 1616 alone.

Land raids were often carried out at night, with the pirates sneaking up on villages, seizing their victims and retreating before the alarm could be sounded. Almost all the inhabitants of the village of Baltimore, in Ireland, were captured in this way in 1631, and attacks on the coast of Devon and Cornwall became a daily feature of life for those people.

The famous diarist Samuel Pepys provided a graphic account of an encounter with two men who'd been taken into slavery, in his diary of 8 February 1661.:

"...to the Fleece tavern to drink and there we spent till 4 a-clock telling stories of Algier and the manner of the life of Slaves there; and truly, Captain Mootham and Mr Dawes (who have been both slaves there) did make me full acquainted with their condition there. As, how they eat nothing but bread and water.... How they are beat upon the soles of the feet and bellies at the Liberty of their Padron. How they are all night called into their master's Bagnard, and there they lie."

Those Europeans unfortunate enough to live closer to North Africa—along the French and Italian coasts, for example, bore the brunt of the white slave traders. They were takne by the thousands from the coasts of Valencia, Andalusia, Calabria and Sicily so often that eventually it was said that "there was no one left to capture any longer."

There are, sadly, no complete records for how many Europeans were captured by the Muslim slavers, but most estimates—based on the size of the Moorish cities—indicate that by 1780, at least 1.2 million Europeans had been seized.

Very few ever managed to escape, and most ended their days dying of starvation, disease, or maltreatment. A tiny number converted to Islam—a way of guaranteeing freedom, as only kuffars were enslaved—and an even smaller number escaped.

This remarkable book, first published in 1693, contains one of the few genuine eye-witness accounts, written by a white slave who managed to escape. Its graphic description of the lot of white slaves, the Moorish relations with the Jews of North Africa, the conditions of the time and the author's eventual escape, cast a dramatic and nowadays, oft-hidden light upon the time when whites were enslaved.

This version has kept the spelling of the time, and the only "change" has been to split the text up into chapters. Otherwise it remains identical to the book which first appeared over 250 years ago.

To Their
Sacred Majesties,
William and *Mary,*
Of *Great-Britain, France* and *Ireland,*
K ING and Q UEEN .

Most Gracious Soveraigns,

AMIDST the throng of those weighty and important Cares that fill your Royal Breasts, it is indeed a high presumption, in one so inconsiderable as I am, to offer the interrupting them by ths Address. But since such is your Royal Clemency, as not to deny Access to the meanest of Your Subjects, Permit me, with awful Reverence and Humility, to lay the ensuing Narrative at Your Majesties Feet, with hopes You will vouchsafe to shelter it under Your Royal Patronage.

The deplorable and miserable Condition, wherein many of Your Majesties Subjects, with other Christians, now lie groaning in Slavery, and under the barbarous Tyranny and Inhumanity of *Mully Ishmael* Emperor of *Morocco,* is a Subject that may perhaps not altogether be thought unworthy of the Cognizance of Your Majesties; it being manifest to all the World how much it has been the Glorious Design of Your Majesties whole Life and Reign, to set Mankind at Liberty, and to free the Distressed from the Yoke of Tyranny and Oppression. May that Almighty Hand that has framed Your Majesties for the Support and Joy of the Universe, continue to Crown all Your Affairs with uninterrupted Success, giving You more and more the Hearts of Your Subjects, and the Necks of Your Enemies. And after Your Majesties have reaped many Harvests of Lawrels, may You plant such an Olive of Peace, under the Branches whereof all *Europe* may for successive Ages rejoice.

Which is and shall be the constant Prayer of Your Majesties poor and distressed, tho Loyal Subject,
Francis Brooks.

TO THE
READER.

Courteous Reader,

THOUGH I must own my self incapable to write upon this Subject, any thing worthy to be exposed to the publick View, since my Eduction hath not given me those Advantages of Stile and Composition, altogether necessary for such an Undertaking: Yet considering I had the miserable Experience of what hath been barbarously inflicted on me, with many others my Fellow Sufferers, who are still groaning under the most insupportable Miseries; I thought my self bound in Duty to publish, as well as I can express it, what was plain Matter of Fact, to the end it might more powerfully move your Compassion, and excite your Charity for the Redemption of those who remain to this Day under their Egyptian Task-masters.

A full Account of which you have in the ensuing Relation, wherein I have made it my Business, to give you a clear and particular View of the most remarkable Passages that happened during the unfortunate time of my Confinement among those barbarous Savages.

I shall offer nothing but Truths, which ten Years Sufferings have made me too long acquainted with. We were not only banished from our Native Country, (being English-men, and my self born in *Ratcliff*-Parish in *Bristol*) but from all the Spiritual as well as Temporal Comforts. We were confin'd amongst those whose Religion was composed of Cruelty, whose Customs were Extravagant, and whose Usages almost Intolerable; what from the hardness of our Labours, and the coarsness of our Provisions, we were reduced to the most pressing Extremities, which caused us to think and contrive all Ways and Means to procure our desired Liberties; which considering how narrowlywe were watch'd, and how closely kept, was almost impossible to be effected.

I need not mention here how I made my Escape, with two others of my Companions, since I have given you an exact Account of it, with all its Circumstances, in the following Relation, with what happened afterwards to the Person who was instrumental in our happy Deliverance, for which we are in Duty bound, during the whole Course of our Lives, to own the particular Providence of God, to whose Assistance and Protection we owe our present Safety.

The chiefest Design of my publishing this Book, is to Caution all Seafaring Men, whose particular Voyages carry them into the *Streights*, that they take all possible care not to be trapan'd by these subtile Pirates who infest those Coasts, where we unfortunately fell into their Hands; and that reflecting on the Barbarities they must expect to suffer from those merciless Enemies, it will be their surest Interest to defend themselves to the utmost of their Power, even to the last Extremity, Death it self being to be preferred before that, or any other Slavery.

Another Motive is, That I hope what I write, may be a Means to procure Liberty for these my Country-men, who are now labouring under the most pressing Miseries, and who would be very serviceable at this Time against the Common Enemy; whose deplorable Condition hath been not long time since published and recommended in a Brief to be continued for two whole Years, as followeth.

William and *Mary*, by the Grace of God, King and Queen of *England, Scotland, France* and *Ireland*, Defenders of the Faith, &c. To all and singular Arch bishops, Bishops, &c.

Whereas a great number of Our good Subjects, peaceably following their Emploments at Sea, have been taken by the Turkish Pirates of *Algiers*, *Salley, Barbary*, and other Places on the Coast of *Africa*, and now remaining Slaves, in Cruel and Inhumane Bondage, without any Days of Rest, either on the Turkish Sabbath or Ours, except four Days in a Year, being kept to extream Labour; from which some endeavourng a little Rest, several of them were barbarously Murdered. Neither is their Diet any more Tolerable than their Labour, great Numbers being allowed no other Food than decayed Barley, which stinketh so that the Beasts refuse to eat it: And often they are not permitted to go from their Labour to fetch Water, which is their only Drink; and sometimes driven about by *Black-a-moors*, who are set over them as Task-masters; and some by them have been so severely whipp'd, that they have dropp'd down Dead.

Whose miserable Conditions being represented to Us, and We having now an Offer from the Emperor of *Fez* and *Morocco*, by his Envoy sent hither to Treat about a general Redemption of all the English that are his Slaves; and the Dey of *Algiers* having now also invited Us to redeem Our Subjects there in Slavery, &c.

So that if the before-recited End may have its desir'd Success, it will make sufficent Amends for any Censures or Reflections that may be made on me, upon the account of my imperfect Performance: therefore I shall only refer their disressed Case to your Benevolence and Charity, as I do my Book to your Pardon and Candour; which, I hope, will neither be denied to them, nor

Your
Humble Servant,
F. B.

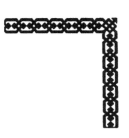

Chapter One: Captured by the Algerines

IN *November* 1681, I went on Board the *William* and *Mary* of *Bristol*, of 120 Tuns Burden, 7 Guns and 4 Paterero's, *William Bowry* Commander, being bound from *Bristol* to *Plymouth* for a Convoy, from whence we went with our Convoy (the *Turkish Tyger*) to *Cales*, where she left us; when the Fleet was safe arrived, we staid there for good Company or Convoy; but none coming, our Merchants went to a French Commander of 26 Guns that was bound for *Marseilles*; who agreed with them to carry us safe thither: In order thereunto he went aboard and fired a Gun, which hearing, we set sail after him.

We were not above three Leagues out of *Cales*, but he hoisted his Top-sails, and left us; however we got safe to*Malaga*, where we again waited for a Convoy: but after we had staid there a considerable time, expecting we should have met with one, we were forced to go without, being loaded with Herrings which were likely to be spoiled.

From thence we went to *Allicant*, where we met with two *Flemings* bound for *Marseilles*, one of 16 Guns, the other of 20, with whom we set Sail about Four a Clock in the Morning: and four hours after we met with the *Bristol* Frigat, who enquired from whence we came? they answered, From *Algier*.

We enquired what was the best News there? they answered, Good News, for they had made Peace with *Algier*; so we brought to, and our Master hoisted out his Boat, and went aboard them, and procured a Copy of the Articles of Peace made between the *English* and *Algerines*: after which he sailed with the two *Flemings* in Company to *Marseilles*, where we lay 19 days for Pratique, which being gained, we went into the Mould and delivered our Loading; after which our Master was very urgent for us to take in our Loading, and so return; but the Merchants said we must wait a while, and we should have it; so we took ino our Ballast, and our Master took in the Merchants at *Santra Pee*: and afterwards we went to *Santra Pell*, and took in Loading of Oil, and set Sail for *Bristol*: but coming homewards, we put into *Malaga*, where there was a Ship that came from *Tunis*, bound for *London*, in which were two Lions and two *Barbary* Horses, being a Present for the late King *Charles* the Second, whose Commander came on board us, to give our Master a Visit. We enquired of him whither he was bound? he said, To *Tangier*, but to make no stay but one day.

Our Master told him he should be glad of his Company homewards: who said he should be likewise glad of his Company; upon which our Master went ashoar, having some Concerns with the Merchants. The same day the *Londoner* sail'd away, leaving us behind. Next day, being the 2d of *August* 1681, in the Morning we set Sail alone; and coming within six Leagues of *Tangier*, we saw a Ship give us chase, when they came up with us, ask'd us whence we came? we said from *Marseilles*.

We enquired the same of her; who answered, From *Algier*: so he bid our Master hoist out his Boat: our Master answered, he would not for any Ship he should meet withal.

Our Master further told him, he should hoist out his Boat if he had any thing to do with him, and if he came to him, he should see he had a Pass; so he sent his Lieutenant aboard us in his own Boat, to whom our Master shewed his Pass, and he acknowledged it to be good, and calling to his Commander, told him the same, who nevertheless desired our Captain to come abord with his Pass: our Master told him, that if the Lieutenant would stay on board us, one of our Men should go aboard, and shew him the Pass.

The Lieutenant agreed thereto, and when the Captain had viewed the Pass, the *Moors* went into their own Ship, and loading their Pistols they stuck them in the Waste-band of their Drawers under their Coats, and every one of them had likewise a Cutlass stuck on their Waste: so they entred aboard us all at once, firing their Pistols, and cut and wounded us with their Cutlasses.[1]

---

[1] When they meet with any of our Merchant-Men of small Force, having but 8 or 10 guns, they often deceive them, by telling them they are *Algerines*, getting the

They had on board them 300 Men and 16 Guns; when they had thus taken our Ship, they carried us to *Sally*, and sent our ship into *Memora*, having secured us in a place under Ground: our Diet they gave us was a little black Bread and Water. There they kept us four days, and then sent us to *Memora* to discharge the Ship they took from us, and sent the Oil with which we were loaden, in Skins, upon Camels and Mules, to the Emperor of *Morocco*.

After we had work'd there very hard all Day in delivering the Ship, they put us down in the Hold of their Ship in Irons, and afterwards sent us to *Macqueness*, where the Emperor's Castle is, and where he keeps all his Slaves, and we were delivered up to the Vice-Roy, (the Emperor being then in Camp against a City to the Southward, called *Tarradant* in *Barbary*) and by his Negroes we were driven to work all day, driving and cursing of us, bidding us turn *Moors*, and at Night we were driven to a place where the rest of the Christians lay, being like a Vault under ground.

Master on board them to shew his Pass; when he and his Men are on board, they enter them, and take their ship.

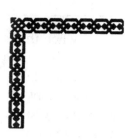

Chapter Two: The Chief of the Jews and Mully Hammet

In the Year 1680, the English Captives that were under this inhuman Tyrant, the Emperor of *Morocco*, bewailing their own Condition, making moan to one another, and praying to God for Deliverance, at last concluded amongst themselves to draw a Petition to our late King *Charles* the Second of *Great Britain*, giving him to understand their miserable Condition in this Captivity: which being done, the King took it into Consideration, and sent over Captain *Francis Nicolson*; who being come, and seeing the Cruel Bondage his poor Country-men were in, their hard Labour and cruel Fare, having therewith many cruel Stripes and Blows, he could not but lament their Condition, and prayed God that he might come to some Composition with that Hellish Tyrant for them.

The Emperor at the same time sent for the Shack, or Chief over all the Jews in his Dominion, and bid him build a Town, which would be better for the Jews than the Cane Houses, (his Name was Abraham Memoran) and at that time Captain *Nicholson* made an Agreement with the Emperor for the Christians, and the *English* and *Portuguese* were delivered him up, the Emperor wishing them a good Journey to *Tangier*; the Captain took them out of the Town that Night, which the Shack of the Jews hearing of, that came to the Emperor, telling him, if he would let him have the Christians to build the Jews Town, he would give him as much Money as the Captain had agreed with him for: the Emperor bid him come again in the morning.

Then the Shack or Chief of the Jews went immediately home to his House, and got a Present ready, and sent it in to the

Emperor's Wife, that she might sollicite the Emperor for him: which having received, she sent word back by the Eunuchs, that she would endeavour to prevail with him, which she did.

And the next Morning he spoke again with the Emperor, who immediately sent out his Negroes to drive back the Christians, which were hurried again to their Works in a cruel manner.

The *Moors* of his City *Maqueness* seeing that, cursed the Jews for doing it: But the Captain could in no wise prevail with this grievous Tyrant the Emperor, (notwithstanding the Captain had done what in him lay to have got the Christians away) who said he would not part with them till the Town was finished.

So they went to work with great Chops, and Baskets to carry Earth in; and the Negroes were set over them to keep them at it from Morning to Night.

When the Town was finished, he put in his Negroes: but the Curse of the Jews fell upon their own Governour, his Mischief returned on his own Head, as will shortly be shewn.

In the mean time the poor Christians were grievously hurried and punished by those Hellish Negroes at the Command of this wicked and inhuman Tyrant the Emperor, and had scarce time to take any Nourishment, or eat any of their bad Bread that was allowed them, but with a great many Threats, Stripes and Blows by the Negroes, bidding them turn *Moors*. In which condition they prayed to God to preserve them in their Faith; in which, through his Assistance, they remained constant.

Sometime after Captain *Nicholson* being gone from thence, the Emperor laid Siege against a City called *Tarradant*, in the South-part of that Dominion, being kept by a King whose Name was *Mully Hammet*: and having been there a considerable time, he sent to the Chief of the Jews, to bring him up some Goods which he wanted from *Maqueness*.

When he had gotten Mules, and carried them to the place where Emperor was in Camp, the Vice-Roy's Son being there with the Emperor, went to the said Shack or Chief of the Jews, and desired him to assist him with some Money, and his Father would repay him, when he, *viz.* the Chief of the Jews, should return to *Maqueness*.

He told him his Father owed him already several thousand Ducats, and would not pay him any, for as yet he could get none from him: and said moreover, if he should die and perish, he would not lend him a penny. Of which Passages he acquainted his Father, writing a Letter thereof to *Macqueness*.

Afterwards the Chief of the Jews went to *Macqueness* to the Vice-Roy called *Coid Birry*, and told him he had acquainted the Emperor of the Care he had in his Absence of his Castle and Business; he taking little notice of him, but returning him Thanks for his Kindness, he went away.

But *Coyd Birry* the Governour (being so called in the Emperor's Absence) ordered one of his chief Negroes in a little time after to go and take such a Horse which he described to him, and go to the place where the Country-People kept their Market, to see if he could find the said Chief of the Jews; and if he saw him, take little notice of him; but if he had an opportunity, watch as he went home to his House, and kill him.

The Negro did as he was ordered, and espying the Shack, or Chief of the Jews, going home to his House, in a Road which lay through a parcel of Olive-Trees, the Negro came to him, pretending Kindness to him, being glad to see him, &c. and riding by his side along on Horseback, spied his opportunity very diligently, so spurred his Horse over him, rode upon him and trode out his Brains.

Word thereof was quickly carried to the Vice-Roy, that the Chief of the Jew was killed, at which he seemed to be sorry, that the People might take no notice thereof, and acquainted the Emperor therewith, and had made search, but knew not who had done it.

The Emperor sent him word back, that if he did not find out who did it, he would cut off his Head, and ordered the said Vice-Roy to put the Governour of the Jews Son to be the Chief in his stead; but the old Jew was soon forgotten by the Emperor.

When the Emperor had laid Siege some Years against *Tarradant*, and could not take it, he returned home to *Macqueness*. After he had been at home a certain time, he went against that City with about 70000 Horse and Foot, and declared that if any Christians knew what belonged to mining, he would set them to work; and that if they took the Town, they should have their Liberty; so four English Men undertook the Work, the *Moors* digged, and they gave Directions.

The Mines being finished, and 30 Barrels of English Powder rowled into the Mine, and a Train laid; the Christian that fired it was blown up: and a Breach was made in the Castle-Wall, but they could not enter, their Enemies fired so thick upon them, killing a great many of *Mully Ishmaell* the Emperor›s Men.

They mined again under the *Burges*, or small Forts: after Powder was put in, and a Train laid, he that gave fire to it, had his Arm struck off, the *Burg* was blown up with the People therein.

And the Emperor *Mully Ishmaell* coming to view the Breach, and being told by the People, the Christian had lost his Arm, he ordered his chiefest Doctor to take care and heal him; for in case he did not see to him carefully, he should lose his Head.

Mully Hammet got up his People to the Breach, and kept out the Emperor and his Forces, that they could not enter. Afterwards *Mully Hammet* went out of his Castle with a small Guard, and meeting with some of the Emperor›s Scouts, one of them knowing *Mully Hammet*, cock'd his Piece and shot him to death: Then *Mully Hammet*'s Guard fought with *Mully Ishmael*'s Scouts, and there were several killed on both sides.

Some of *Mully Hammet*'s Guards retired into the Castle, and acquainted the chiefest of them that were in the Castle, that their King was killed: presently they proclaimed *Mulle Rann* (being the chiefest of the Governours in *Mully Hammet*'s time) to be their King.

Which News being carried to the Emperor by his Scouts, he enquired who had killed *Mully Hammet*? they told him one of the Scouts, which he sent presently for by a Messenger, and bid him acquaint him that he should have a good Reward for killing him; he being brought before the Emperor, expecting a great Reward for so doing, after he had examin'd him, he rewarded him with calling of him Dog, and said he should die for killing *Mully Hammet*, and immediately caused him to be made fast to a Mule's Tail, and so had him dragged through the Camp, and ordered one to go before and declare, that it was for killing of *Mully Hammet*; he was dragged so long till his Body was torn in pieces; after that he had him put in a place where the Country People used to come into the Camp.

Mully Ran kept the Castle and City, and the Emperor›s Forces made more Mines in order to take the City and Castle, which being finished, they blew up the Town-Walls, and severall small Forts, with the People in them, and made so great a Breach that *Mully Ishmaell* entred his Men and took both the City and Castle, and promised the People he would be kind to them: but when he took the Town, he secured their Arms, Ammunition and Treasure, and carried the People of that Place to *Maqueness*: and being come down to *Macqueness*, he put all the Christians, and several hundreds of the Natives to work there to make a Court, and Houses for his Women.

And coming on a certain time, (as he uses constantly to do) although it rained very fast, as he was going into one of the Houses, the Master-Workman and his Assistants going to hoist up a piece of Timber, and the Rope that held it broke, and the Timber fell, with which he suddenly retired back, and sent for the Master-Workman in great Passion, threatning him for taking no better care: he told him he was as careful as he could be for his Life in doing it, saying, it was a Mischance he could not prevent; nevertheless he took a Piece out of one of his Boys Hands, and shot him to Death, and went among the Christians raving and tearing as if he would have killed them all, setting his Negroes and Guard to beat both the *Moors* and the Christians that were at work; which they did with such Violence, that many of them had their Heads and Arms miserably broken, making his Buildings more like a Slaughter-house than a place of Work; and at the same time ran two of his *Moors* through with his Launce.

So that he makes no more to kill a Man at his Pleasure, than to kill a Dog.

In a little time after the Emperor was come to *Macqueness*, the three Christians that were Miners, desired their Liberty as he had promised: He granted it, and ordered a Letter to the Governour of *Sally*, that he should send them away by the first opportunity; a Ship being ready, they desired their Liberty, being at *Sally*, in order for their Journey; but the Governour instead of granting it, abused and railed on them, saying, they should pay him so much a Head, or they should not go.

The English Man that lost his Arm, turned back and acquainted the Emperor thereof, telling him what the Governour said, who wrote a Letter and sent him with two of his chief Negroes, saying, If he would not let them go off, he would cut off his Head: The Governour hearing that, durst not detain them any longer. So the three English Men, whose Names were *William Chalender*, *Robert Jackson*, and *Benjamin Newman*, through the Goodness of God arrived at *London*, and came again to their own Country

Chapter Three: The White Virgin and "That Barbarous and Inhuman Crew"

In the Year 1683, Captain *Venetia* the younger, a Pirate belonging to *Sally*, met with one Mr. *Bellamy*, an English-Man, who was bound for *Leghorn* in a Pink of 8 Guns, to whom he gave Chase: and when he came up to Mr. *Bellamy*, the Pirate examined him from whence he came? he answered, From *London*; and enquired likewise of him whither he was bound? who said, To *Leghorn*.

Mr. *Bellamy* asked him from whence he came, and what Place he belonged to? he said, To *Algier*. The Pirate commanded *Bellamy* to hoist out his Boat, and bring his Pass aboard, who answered, he should hoist out his own if he had any business with him, which he did, and sent his Lieutenant aboard on *Bellamy*.

One of Mr. *Bellamy*'s Men that had been a Captive in *Sally*, knowing the said Pirate, told the Master he knew him very well, and that he belonged to *Sally*.

When the Lieutenant came to *Bellamy*'s side, Mr. *Bellamy* placed some of his Men with their small Arms at the entring, and said, one Man should not enter him save the Lieutenant, who viewed Mr. *Bellamy*'s Pass, acknowledging it to be good.

The Lieutenant returning aboard their own Ship, acquainted the Captain, saying, We'll fire at them and affright them; in order to which, he commanded them to make ready; the Pirate firing at Mr. *Bellamy*, he fired at them again, so they fought a considerable time: Mr. Bellamy killed and wounded about thirty of his Men, and he wounded some of *Bellamy*'s Men: but for want of Powder Mr. *Bellamy* was forced to yield.

When *Venetia* had taken him and his Company, and brought them aboard his own Ship, leaving several of his own Men in their stead, he began to examine Mr. *Bellamy* why he had killed and wounded so many of his Men?

Who answered, he would have killed all the rest, and him too, if he had had Powder; with that the Pirate cut him down with his Cutlass, and rip'd him open, and said, there was an end of a Dog, so threw his murdered Body into the Sea, and carried all his Men into *Sally*, and from thence to *Macqueness*.

Thus have these bloody Heathenish Crew deceived many of our Country-men, telling them they belonged to *Algier*, when they belonged to *Sally*.

I pray God keep all my Country-men, and all good Christians out of the Hands of that barbarous and inhuman Crew, the worst that live upon the Earth! and that all may beware of them, hath caused me thus to write; being one that by sad Experience, and from a certain Knowledg I have had of them, can assure these things to be nothing but a real Truth; and bless God, that he has thought me worthy to escape them, and that I am now come safe to the Land of my Nativity.

In the Year 1685, a Ship being bound from *London* to *Barbadoes*, in which were four Women, two of them being Mother and Daughter; one of those Heathenish Pirates meeting them, gave them Chase, and coming up to them, examined them strictly from whence they came, and whither bound? who told them as afore, From *London* to *Barbadoes*; (the Pirate was *Venetia* the younger, who had 300 Men, and 18 Guns) after the Commander had enquired the same of them, he understood what they were, they telling him, that they came from *Algier*; so they demanded of him to shew his Pass, and said he must hoist out his Boat; they seeing him not provided with Guns to defend himself, could make no Resistance, which being done, the Captain of the Pirate took them into his Cabin, and would shew himself kind to them, treating them, and giving them Dates.

In the mean while the Lieutenant and *Moors* girded their Pistols and Cutlasses on their Wastes, and with the English-man's Boat went aboard his Ship, and took all that were aboard him, with the four Women.

And the Captain asked who the young Woman was, and whether she was ever married? Account being given him concerning her, he ordered her to be put in the Cabin, lest any of his own barbarous Crew should offer to lie with her, and so sailed away for *Sally*.

Being come there, the Captain of the Pirate brought them they had taken to *Macqueness*, and the Women were carried before the Eunuchs. The Captain giving an account to the chief Eunuch, that one of those Women was a Virgin; but for the Men, they were driven by the Negroes to hard Labour.

And afterwards all the Christians of the Ship and the 4 Women were brought up to *Macqueness*; the Women were brought before the Emperor's Eunuchs, and an account given to the Chief of them by the *Moors* Captain, that one of them was a Virgin, and she was immediately sent to the Emperor's Women: and the Eunuch sent to the Vice-Roy, acquainting him how he had disposed of the Virgin, who ordered the other Women to be brought to his House, and ordered the Negroes to drive the poor Christians to hard Labour, who at Night were lock'd up amongst the other Christian Captives, having no Sustenance allowed them for that day; and what their poor Brethren offered them, they could not eat, being such Bread as I have already described, so bad, that the Beasts in that place refused to eat it: and what betwixt their Diet and Lodging on the cold ground, together with the Negroes hard Usage, many of them fell sick.

And to add to their Extremity, were threatned and abused by the Negroes to turn *Moors*; but they daily prayed to God to strengthen them in their Afflictions, and in his great Mercy work some way for their Deliverance out of this dreadful Bondage.

Afterwards the chief Eunuch sent word to the Emperor, that he had a Christian Virgin amongst the rest of his Women. The Emperor ordered him to send her up to the Camp, with a parcel of his Eunuchs to guard her thither.

When she came to the Camp, the Emperor urged her, tempting her with Promises of great Rewards if she would turn *Moor*, and lie with him. She earnestly desired of the Lord to preserve and strengthen her to resist his earnest Perswasions, and great Proffers, which he used, to have his Desires fulfilled.

When he could not prevail so, he fell to threatning her, and put her amongst his Negro Women, and threatned to kill them if they offered to shew her any Kindness, where they kept her, beating and abusing her for several days.

She prayed still to the Lord to strengthen her, and held a Resolution to withstand him; who again sought to prevail with her, tempting and promising of her great things, if she would turn, which she still refused: so he caused her to be stript, and whipt by his Eunuchs with small Cords, so long till she lay for dead; and he caused her to be carried away out of his Presence that time, and charged his Women none of them should help her till he sent for her, which was not till two days after, and in the mean time to have no Sustenance but that black rotten Bread: at which time he sought again to prevail with Promises and Threats, which she still withstood, praying to the Lord that she might be preserved from him, and be delivered from his cruel Hands.

Then he prick'd her with such things, as commonly his Women use instead of Pins, being as sharp. Thus this beastly and inhuman Wretch by all ways he could invent, sought to force her to yield, which she resisted so long, till Tortures, and the hazards of her Life forced her to yield, or resign her Body to him, tho her Heart was otherwise inclined.

So he had her wash'd, and clothed her in their fashion of Apparel, and lay with her; having his Desire fulfilled, he inhumanly, in great haste forc'd her away out of his Presence; and she being with Child, he sent her by his Eunuchs to *Macqueness* (who delivered her with the Emperor's Charge concerning her) to the chief Eunuch, and after that she was delivered of two Children.

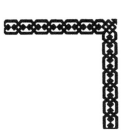

Chapter Five: The Attempted Escape

About four Years ago, two English-men and a French-man being at *Memora*; and as they were passing along the River, on a certain time in a Boat, with some *Moors*, one of which was a Lieutenant, he ordered the Christians to go on Shore to fetch a little of their black Rusk and Water: And as they were passing along the River to take their Pleasure, the Christians said one to another, Now is the time, with the Lord's leave, for us to see for our Liberty.

The French-man said, The *Moors* would be too many for them. The English-men said, Fear not, let us trust in the Lord, and he'll deliver us. So they going aboard with their Bread and Water, the Lieutenant bid them get out their Oars, and pull up like Dogs as they were; which they bore patiently.

At Night some of the *Moors* lying down, they fell upon those *Moors* that were awake. They then fearing the *Christians* would be too hard for them, called out, and awaked the other *Moors*. Then the Lieutenant and other *Moors* came, and he drew his Knife, and stabb'd one of the *English-men* to death, the other knock'd him down, and they fought so long till Blood was spilt on both sides.

The next day the *English-man* and *French-man* were carried up to *Macqueness* in Irons, before the Emperor, and by the *Moors* was informed of what was done. The Emperor upon Examination, told them if they did not immediately turn *Moors*, he would kill them. The *French-man* yielded: the Emperor then threatned the *English-man*, if he did not turn, he would quickly kill him.

He made Answer, God's Power was greater than the Devil's; and let him do what he would, he should not make him turn *Moor*.

The Emperor called for his Sword, and immediately fell to cutting him, threatning him still to turn; he said he was brought up in the Faith of Jesus Christ, and he would not forsake it.

Then this inhuman Wretch in great spleen cut him till he fell down, and hack'd and hewed him as if he had been butchering an Ox, and caused the Negro Boys to run his Body full of Holes with Knives, till his Body was as full of Holes as possible it could be; when he had so done, Bring, saith he in his own Language, four English Dogs to fetch that Dog away: and as they carried his Body away, the Negro Boys stoned them, saying, that should be the end of them if they did not turn *Moors*; but they were glad to go quietly without answering again; if they had made any Reply, they had certainly been fallen upon by the Negro Boys.

So their greatest Satisfaction was, his dying in the Christian Faith, and his counting that more precious than his own Life, holding the same stedfast before that cruel Tyrant, whilst he had Breath in his Body.

Then they carried him to the place where they lodged under ground, so took off his Irons and kept him there all Night, and the next Morning carried him where he was to be buried, the Negroes still stoning of them as they went along. As soon as they had laid his Body in the Ground, they were hurried by the Negroes to work again after their usual manner.

The Tyrant coming a certain time to view his Work, examining what was the reason they went no faster on? They answered, Several of the Christians were fallen sick: So this inhuman Tyrant went to the place where they lay, which was under Ground (acting the part of *Herod*, in killing at his Pleasure, as well as of *Pharaoh*, who of old encreased the Israelites Bondage, in causing them to make Brick, and allowing them no Straw. But we read of the End of those cruel Tyrants.)

So by the Emperor's Order his Negroes fell to haling and dragging them out of that place, when in that weak and feeble condition that they could not stand on their Legs when dragged before him; he instantly killed seven of them, making their Resting-place a Slaughter-house. The very *Moors* were terrified to see so inhuman and bloody an Action.

Chapter Six: The Tyrant's Building Works

It is a Proverb, *The more Rain, the more Rest*: but God knows it was most commonly our Lot to be driven and kept closest at our Work when it rained; yea, when it rained most fast, our Work was nothing lessened, but the more encreased: and besides the Christians, he sets thousands of his own Natives to work with great Chops, and to carry Earth on their Heads in Baskets from one place to another.

And let it rain never so fast, (there falling store of Rains in the Winter Season) he'll stay by them, setting his Negroes to drive them with Whips of small Cords and Sticks from Morning till Night; and if he's minded to eat, he often sends home to his Castle, and hath his Victuals sent him, lest the Slaves should neglect his Work.

He hath great Buildings in his Castle, which will not be finished in his time, and there he keeps the poor People at work, in order to suppress and keep them low.

His small Forts at his Castle are more for a show of great Strength, to make his Enemies afraid, than for any use he puts them to, making them into Store-houses, and turning them to such-like uses.

In the Year 1688, the Tyrant coming out one time to see his Works, as constantly he did, a sort of stuff they used instead of Mortar, being Earth, Lime, and Sand mixed together, to build their Walls with; and taking up a handful thereof, he did not like it: upon which he sent his Negroes to fetch the Master-Workman to him, which being haled by the Neck before him, he asked why more Lime was not mixt with the Earth?

He made answer he wanted Lime, and that was the reason the Stuff was no better: he sent for the Shack of the Negroes and Christians that were at work, examining him after the same manner? who said he wanted Mules to bring them Lime: he then sent for the Mules to see how many there were, and wanting one of his number, which the Negro said he had at his House, and was lame, he ordered his Negro Boys to keep him fast, while he sent some of the rest to enquire whether the Negro said true? but they finding not the Mule that was wanting, he ordered the Negro, immediately to be stript unto his Drawers, and fastened to a Mule's Tail, which was done, and he was dragg'd so the space of half a Mile to Prison, there to remain; and had the Master-Workman stretch'd out by four Negroes, two at his Hands and two at his Feet, beating of him till he could not turn himself, bidding him take care of his Mules, saying, if when he came again he found such bad stuff for his Work, he would cut off his Head.

So immediately he sent his Negro Boys to fetch the seventy Christians that were at hard Labour making a Wall; so asked one of them if he could speak his Language? who said he could, examining him in like manner about the Stuff? who answered, he durst not for fear acquaint him of the Badness of it: so, he took one of his Sticks they used to carry after him, and calling him Dog, bid him hold his Head fare to strike at: having strucken him down, he knocked down all the rest with his own Hands, and broke their Heads so miserably, that the place was all bloody like a Butcher's Stall, and none of them durst make Resistance, for if they had, he would presently have killed them.

So he bid them rise like Dogs as they were, saying, if they used any more such bad Stuff in his Work, he would kill them all.

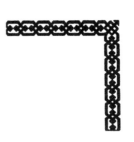

Chapter Seven: The Exchange of Moors for Christians

In 1689, the Emperor sent down to the Coyde, or Governour of *Tangier*, to take a view of *Alarache*, where was a Garison belonging to the King of *Spain*. The Governour taking view thereof, he sent him farther Orders to prepare for the taking it, if he could possibly. So sending back to the Emperor to provide him Forces, the Emperor sent him down 40000 Horse and Foot, besides the Forces he had there: And he laying Siege to the Place, the Spanish Boats fetch'd off the Officers Wives and Children.

They afterwards raised a small Fort, to keep all small Vessels or Boats from fetching any Thing off. Which the Friars taking notice of, hoisted up a Flag of Truce; and came to a Treaty with the Governour of the *Moors*, till they had been with the Emperor at *Macqueness*.

When come thither, they told him, that if he would let them go, and take what was their own with them, they would give him the Place, with the Christians, and all the Ammunition and Guns. To which he agreed, saying, He would.

They returning again to *Alarach*, ordered the Governour of the *Moors* to make a Feast; and going to their own Garison, told their own Governour, that they had made an Agreement with the Emperor, and that they should march into *Ceuta* in their own Arms, saying, They had better do so, than go into Slavery amongst the Christians.

The Governour, and the Governour of the King of *Spain* dining together: When Dinner was over, he bid him send for his Men, and send them with all speed to *Ceuta*. They being come, he commanded them to lay down their Arms; which he (to wit, the *Moors* Governour) quickly secured, telling them, they must go up to the Emperor at *Macqueness*, for he had a mind to see them, and afterwards they must return to *Ceuta*.

So the *Moors* took the great Guns, with their Carriages, Muskets and Powder, carrying them all to the Emperor, with a Band of Men to guard them thither. Being come thither, he set his Negroes to drive them to work; ordering the great Guns to be unmounted, and laid flat on the Ground betwixt the two Walls, with those Guns that were brought from *Memora*.

So the Negroes kept them at hard Slavery, beating and whipping them all day long; and at Night they were to lodge underground; allowing them such Bread as his other poor Captives have, and Water to sustain them alive.

After the poor Christians had undergone their hard Labour and cruel Stripes, for the space of five Months time, many of them fell sick and died: then this Tyrant came and enquired, what was become of them? they gave him account, that seven hundred of them were turned *Moors*, and five hundred were dead.

After that the poor *Christians* concluded to draw a Petition to the King of *Spain*, and lay before him their miserable Condition under this Tyrannical Emperor, having but now and then rotten Bread, and Water when they could catch it, and therewith cruelly punished to add to their Extremity. The King of *Spain* received their Petition; and viewing it, declared to his Council what a Condition his poor Subjects were in under this cruel Tyrant the Emperor of *Morocco*.

And the said King took it into consideration, and sent over an Ambassador to the Emperor, to see if he could agree with him for his Subjects that were there in Slavery. The Ambassador being come, an Agreement was made betwixt them, that the King of *Spain* should give a thousand *Moors* for an hundred *Christians*.

And for the Souldiers Wives that were not carried off, and young Children, they agreed for 4 *Moors* a Head. The Ambassador bargained with the Emperor, to have the *Christians* down to *Tittivan*, lying near unto *Tangier*, and there to remain till the *Moors* were brought over, and left at *Ceuta*, a Place not far from thence.

After which the Ambassador returned home to the King of *Spain*, acquainting his Master what a miserable Condition his poor

Subjects were in, working from Morning to Night, allowing them nothing but old rotten Barley-bread and Water; not suffering them to have any thing to lie upon, after their hard Labour and cruel Usage by the *Moors*, nor no Apparel to wear, but daily beating them, and often with his own Hands, to force them to turn *Moors*.

The King of *Spain* ordered his Ambassador to take as many *Moors* as he had agreed for: So he went and got the *Moors* together, and went over to *Ceuta* with them; when being come thither, he went to *Tittivan*; and leaving the *Moors* in *Ceuta*, he spoke to their Governor, told him the *Moors* were ready at *Ceuta*, and that as many *Christians* as he was pleased to send to *Ceuta*, there should be so many *Moors* surrendred as they had agreed for.

When the *Moors* were all delivered up, and the *Christians* brought in; The *Moors* Governour brought them up to *Maqueness* to the Emperor; the Emperor enquired of them how they had fared in Christendom?

They answered, they had allowed them a Jacket and a pair of Breaches once a Year; and for their Provision, they had a certainty of Rusk, and hot Beans once a Day.

But being come to their own Country, they began to lament the Christian Captives poor Condition, seeing daily what they endured with Hunger, Cold and Stripes; and many times the Tears fell from their Eyes for Grief to see it; some of the *Moors* saying, We are *Christians*, (privately to them) but durst not publickly own it: And at another time told the Captives, (when they saw the Emperor's Cruelty, often murdering one or other at his Pleasure; and themselves had nothing allowed them but a little of that rotten Barley-bread, and a little Butter than stunk) that they had rather be in *Spain* than there.

And some of the *Moors* got back again into *Spain*, acquainting the People there what a cruel Tyrant their Emperor was, and how miserably he used the poor Christians.

And when the Spanish Ambassador returned with the *Christians*, into their own Country, the King asked them how they had fared? Who gave a large Account, as aforesaid, of the hard Bondage and Slavery the Emperor of *Morocco* had kept them in whilst they were under him.

The King said, it was well they had kept their Faith, as they had done, whilst there. And his Ambassador drew a Petition to the

King his Master, imploring his Favour to remember them that were left behind, and take their suffering Condition into his Christian Consideration; which he did, and ordered them some Relief.

Those that were left behind, likewise petitioned him to allow them something Yearly: Which was done, and care taken that it should be sent over for their Use: As likewise our Factories at *Cales* and *Portugal*, having enquired how it was with them; and understood the English fared no better than the rest, contributed towards their Necessities, and sent it over from *Cales* to *Tittivan*, to one Mr. *Anthony Packer* a Merchant there, desiring him to order it them for their Relief: Who accordingly did, and they therewith bought them a few Clothes to cover their Nakedness.

So they wrote back to Mr. *Anthony Packer*, and to the Factories, returning them Thanks for their Kindness in remembring them, praying to God to prosper them in their Affairs. And I beseech God to open the Hearts of our Gracious King and Queen of *England*, as he hath done others, to grant some Relief for their distressed Subjects that are yet in that place, whose cruel Sufferings I could do no less than acquaint them with, being when I left them, in as poor a condition as ever.

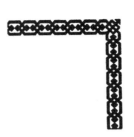

Chapter Eight: The Condition of the Christian Captives

The poor Christian Captives that are taken by any of those Hellish Pirates belonging to the Emperor of *Morocco*, are brought up to *Macqueness*, being kept at hard Work from Day-light in the Morning till Night, carrying Earth on their Heads in great Baskets, driven to and fro with those barbarous Negroes by the Emperor's Order: and when they are drove home by the Negroes at Night to their Lodging, which is on the cold Ground, in a Vault or hollow place in the Earth, laid over with great Beams a-thwart, and Iron Bars over them, they are told in there like Sheep, and out in the Morning; and if any be wanting, he quickly secures the Negroes, and sends out a parcel of his Guard to look for them.

Their Food is Bread made of old rotten Barley, and their Drink Water when they can get it: Many times when they are hurried to their Work in a Morning, not knowing whether they shall be able to undergo their Afflictions till Night: and when they are drove home, expecting Rest, the Tyrant sends some of his Negroes to hurry them again to work, either to hale down Walls, cut Gates, or the like, keeping them both Night and Day many times without either Bread or Water, which is all their Sustenance: when they have done that, the Negroes dare not to drive them home before he gives order, lest they be killed for so doing; when they have his Order, they drive them home, tell them over, and so lock them up until Day-light in the Morning.

And in this Captivity I have been, with the rest of my poor Country-men for the space of Ten Years, being so long since taken; but now, through the Mercies of God, I am come to see my Native Country, and cannot but condole their Miseries I have left behind under that cruel Tyrant the Emperor of *Morocco*; beseeching Almighty God, that none of my Country-men may ever come to have a share under that hard Task-Master.

There are three hundred and forty *English-men*, Subjects of our Gracious King, in this sore Captivity.

Chapter Nine: The Nature of the Tyrant

This Emperor, as I have been informed, touching his Birth or Descent, was begotten of a Negro Woman by a white Man, one of the noblest of their Quality in that time, and is a *Mollatto* by his Colour; but when he's in a Passion, he looks just as he is, as black as an Infernal Imp; which his Natives take notice of, and can tell when he's angry.

For his Apparel, he wears a fine Holland Shirt, with Sleeves so large that will make any ordinary Man a pair of Drawers, besides a large pair of Drawers of the same, with Breeches over them, and next to his Shirt a Garment of as Fine Stuff as can be had, made of the fashion of a Wastcoat without Sleeves, and over that a Coat of as fine Cloth as can be bought, made almost of our fashion; he wears over that a sort of Garment which they call a *Shilham*, or *Barnoose*, but we may call it a short Cloak, being wrought all over with Silver and Gold, with a Cap to go over his Head, having at the top of it a great Bob with a Fringe, and at the bottom a great Fringe all round it: on the lower part from his Breast it is open, and the upper part made fast; and over that in cold Weather he wears a Cloak, with a Cap to put over his Head: upon his Head he wears sometimes a Turbet (as they call it) made of Silk; and when it is hot Weather, he wears a Garment made of a sort of Stuff like fineCrape, and a Hat; and on his Legs he wears fine red Boots, but different from our Fashion: he's oftner on Horse-back than on Foot; his Guard, which are of different Stature, wear some of them Shoes, and have over their Shirts and Drawers only Cloaks with Caps, some light coloured, and some dark: sometimes he has an hundred following him, and at other times fifty, and sometimes more, he having thirty thousand Negroes of his own Slaves.

Every one of his black Guard have a Piece, and he has three or four Launces carried after him, and several Pieces ready charged; to kill with at his Pleasure either the Christians or his own Natives.

When he falls out with his Guards, he strips and takes their Clothes, from them and puts them in Irons, and sets them to work. He seldom returns home after his going out in a Morning, without killing one or other before he returns, by running of them through with his Launce, shooting them, or dragging them at a Mule's Tail, either Men or Women, seldom repenting for what he has done; *Mahomet* their great Prophet possessing them with a Belief, that if he kills any one, he merits Heaven by so doing; but if any Person should kill him, he cannot avoid going to Hell.

He has Water carried after him by a Boy, which he drinks, to make the People believe he drinks nothing else; and likewise short Sticks carried after him daily, to beat the poor Slaves at his Pleasure, which is hourly, to vex and punish them, delighting in nothing more.

He was first made a *Coyde* or Governour of some part of the Country, and by his Kindness and Affability to the People, he gained Respect from them in that Country. *Mully Sheade* being then King, and living in the City of *Fez*, there died; and the Inhabitants there being all *Whites*, and he a *Mollato*, they cried up *Mully Hammet*.

Mully Ishmael being then beloved of his own People, he raised a small Army, and went against the said City and won it; having conquered *Fez*, he still strove to oblige the People; and one *Guillan* raised a small Army, against whom *Mully Ishmael* went. *Guillan* being a great Friend to our Nation, the Governour of *Tangier* offered him Assistance if he was pleased to accept it: he returned him Thanks, saying, it was bad enough for himself and his own Army to be conquered, and it would be worse for the Christians if they should go with him; but engaging himself, *Mully Ishmael* conquered him, and his People carried his Head up to *Macqueness*.

When I was there, the Emperor kept two of *Guillan*'s Sons in his Castle, and had them at School amongst his own Children, because of their Father's Courage and Stoutness. Our English Governour was concerned at the loss of *Guillan* and his People. When the Emperor had won most of his Country, and conquered *Tarradant*, he soon after came to *Macqueness*, and ordered all his Bashaws or Governours to build Walls and great Houses upon their own Charge, on pain of losing their Lives. Some finished their Houses, and some could not, having not wherewith to do it, being brought so low, he causing it to be so, that they might not rebel against his chief Son called *Mully Sedan*, for whom he hath the greatest Esteem above all his Sons, thinking he may succeed after his Decease: but I hope in God, and wish it may never be, for the young Tyrant imitates his Father too much in cutting and killing the Slaves as bad as he almost; that the People begin to dread him as well as the old one.

The Emperor's Castle hath four Gates belonging to it. The City of *Macqueness* is an old decay'd place, the Castle standing distant from it, and walled in some places double, and has a few old Iron Guns mounted upon them: For the Brass Guns that were taken from the King of *Spain*, he's afraid to leave them with any of his Governours, lest they rise against him, and had them brought up to *Macqueness*, plac'd within the Castle Gates betwixt two Walls flat upon the Ground.

The Buildings within the Walls are very high, and several small Forts round the Castle-Walls. And lately he set the People to build two new towns, (with which to plague his Country People, to bring them as low as he can) which I think will never be finished in his time; and if he did it on his own Cost and Charge, he would not have so many Buildings. When Taxes are brought him in, he treasures it up, taking but little out again.

The common Diet the Emperor uses to eat, is made like a kind of Grain; they call it *Cuscozoo*, being boiled and mixed with their Butter, which is far more loathsome and strong to us than our Butter in *England*; being put into Platters, they put thereon Mutton cut in small pieces.

So he sits down, and thrusting his Hand into it, he shakes it a little to and fro, crambing it in his Mouth together. When he has done, he calls his Negroes to take what's left to eat while he stands over them, and they are in great fear lest he kill them; which he certainly would do, if one should eat more than another.

Their Drink is commonly Water; 'tis said, he'l drink Wine; wherein he makes invalid the Doctrine of their great Prophet

Mahomet, who told the People, It was a great Sin to do it; yea, and he'l often be drunk too, (to the sorrow of his poor Slaves); though if any of the rest, if it be the greatest among them, be found in the like Case, if he comes to the knowledg of it, he'l kill them.

His Guards about him are made up of Negro Boys, of fourteen, sixteen, or eighteen Years old. If he calls for the greatest Man in his Country about the least Crime, they presently run like so many Hounds; and they come Collering of him, as if he were a Bullock to be slaughtered: When he's hal'd so before the Emperor, he either kills him, or he's beaten, or put in Irons, and thrown into Prison; and after this manner he governs his own People.

When he had Business with our Nation, and asked Advice of the Chief of his own Country, none durst say his Concern would go Well or Ill, for fear he would dislike what they said, although he would often require them to do it: So he first gives his own Judgment of the Matter, and they say as he does.

He is seldom true to his Word, having cheated most Kings and Princes that have any thing to do with him; as in the Case of the *Algerines*, who made him pay dearly for it.

Whilst I was there, he made Peace with *Holland* and *France*; but soon broke it, taking since that time several Dutch and French Ships, making Slaves of their Subjects. If he swears one thing to Day, he'l swear quite another on the Morrow.

Yet he did not out-wit (notwithstanding his Falshood and Treachery) the King of *Spain*'s Ambassador, who surrendred not one of the *Moors*, till the *Christians* were got into the Spanish Garison.

If any Christian King or Prince sends an Ambassadour to this Emperor, (as in my Time there have been from *England, Spain* and *France*) when they come thither, he makes them wait a considerable time: And he's so high in his own Conceit, that except they be Persons of Quality, he regards them not; and when they come before him, he'l be either in his Stable, or on Horseback, or sitting on an heap of Earth, and so speaks to them by an Interpreter, (and he will not allow a Penny towards their Charges, nor any Place to lodg in, be they who they will) and so sends for several of the White-men, being Bashaws or Governours, the chiefest of his Country, who dare not for their Lives be Judges to speak otherwise than what he says first, for fear of him.

About twelve Years since, he sent an Ambassdour over to our late King *Charles* the Second, to Congratulate his Majesty, and Treat with him for Peace, or the like; and in the mean time sent out his Pirats to take our English Ships.

Our King not thinking him to be so false, sent him a Present over by *Hammet Benkado* the Emperor's Ambassador; who is now as barbarous to the poor *Christians*, as any belonging to the Emperor.

He never goes to rest, but when dead Sleep overcomes him, and make him so drowsy, that he can't hold up his Head; and as he goes to rest, he often kills one or other of his Negroes, at home as well as abroad.

Then in one of his Rooms in the Castle, he lies down on a kind of Quilt on the Ground; and sleeping that Night, he rises early in the Morning, and falls to his old Tyrannous and Inhumane Practices, domineering over his poor Slaves, and sets the Negroes to whip, stone and beat them, to work harder than many times it's possible for them to think they can hold out or endure till Night.

The poor Christians, the English Captives, daily praying to God, if it be his Will, to support them in this distressed Condition, and to keep them and deliver them from under this miserable Oppression they are under, and restrain the Hands of that bloody Tyrant: And when they think of their Native Country, and the Government thereof, they cannot but greatly lament their own Condition, erecting their Prayers to Heaven for the Preservation of their own King and Country; and that God would be pleased to open their Hearts to remember them in this sad and deplorable Condition.

Thus bemoaning one another, they commit their Case to him, who is the wise Disposer and Orderer of all things, without whose Permission nothing can be acted or done, who can in his due Time grant them Relief.

On Fridays the Emperor goes to his Place of Worship, having first viewed his Slaves, being of several sorts, both *Christians*, *Negroes*, and a sort of People called *Brabboes*; the last sort being Natives of the Country, which he suppresseth so much, that they are not able to pay him Taxes, keeping them at as hard Slavery as the rest.

If he kills none in the Morning before he goes to Worship, they dread him for fear he will at his return: he rides thither and back again, going about Eleven of the Clock, and returns about One, against which time the poor Slaves order one or another to watch, and are in as great fear when they see him as if they must all be destroyed; and they all work more hard that day than all the rest of the Week.

He killed seven and twenty *Moors* on one day; but there's none can tell the several thousands of poor Souls this unmerciful Tyrant hath slain since his Reign, which is now about two and twenty Years.

For his Women I think he knows not the number of them, he hath so many, both *Whites*, *Blacks*, *Mollatoes*, and *Copper-colour'd*; and for Apparel they have a piece of Silk of a Red or Yellow Colour, which they wear over their Heads.

They wear Shifts or Smocks made of fine Linnen, big enough to make two Shifts, and fine Drawers that will reach down to their Heels, which are open or slit in the middle; and their upper Garment is fine Flannel, and a Silk Girdle about their middle: upon each of their Breasts they wear Silver or Gold Pins, with which they fasten their upper Garment; and upon the Wrists of their Hands they wear on each a Silver Shackle, and likewise upon the Small of their Legs; and on their Feet red Slippers.

He hath store of Children of several Colours. He hath built within his Castle fine Dwellings for himself to live and lodg in; and for his Women he hath built very fine Houses, two Courts very sumptuous; in the bigger of them are seventy two Marble Pillars, each at least three foot thick, to support the fine painted Works above; in the middle of the greater Court is a Marble Cistern with curious Spring-Water, which springs or boils up in the middle thereof, and comes from a Fountain about two Miles from the Castle.

If he desires to lie with any of his Women, he sends an Eunuch to fetch whom he pleases: she being come, he lies with her, after that he bids her begone; being as inhumane in this as in the rest of his Actions; and away she goes, lest he kill her.

He allows his Women a quantity of Flour, and sends his Eunuchs to measure it them out; and sometimes goes to look over them himself, lest his Eunuchs cheat him.

One of his Women came to him carrying a young Child in her Arms, desiring him to allow her a little more Flour and Butter; he bid her stay a while, and she should have it; then he called for some of his Eunuchs, and killed her, and caused them to pull the young Child in pieces Limb from Limb.

It's his Pleasure sometimes to shew his Women his fine Buildings: before he goes, he sends his Eunuchs to drive away all the Men out of their sight, riding with a Lance himself before the Women, being two or three hundred following, where he rides in great Pomp, extolling this and the other Work, and admiring the Bravery thereof; but the Women dare not to speak a word otherwise than as he himself doth.

Chapter Ten: Conflict with the Algerines

In the Year 1688, the Emperor of *Morocco* sent a Letter to the *Algerines*, acquainting them that he heard they had a great many Christian Slaves; and since he had a great deal of Work to do, if they would sell him any of them, he would give them 150 Dollars a Head for five hundred of them, and send them away with all speed.

They gathered three hundred French Men, and brought them to *Tittivan*; being landed there, the Governour had them to *Macqueness* to the Emperor, to see them, and asked him if he liked them? who answered, Yes.

Immediately by the Emperor's Order they were driven away by the Negroes in a barbarous manner. The *Algerines* expecting their Money from the Emperor, having waited a long time for Payment, they resolved at once to demand it from him.

When they asked him for it, he answered, he did not use to give Money for Christians that were brought into his Land. Then they charged him with breach of Promise, saying, they hoped he would not serve them so.

He said, if they did not retire out of his Country, he would cut off all their Heads. So they retiring to *Algier* with speed, acquainted the King and his Pateroons how they had sped with the Emperor, giving Relation of what he said concerning the Christians.

The King presently rais'd an Army of 50000 Men, preparing Ammunition and Field-pieces, who marched through *Trimsind*, a place at or near the Emperor's Dominions, where they entred without Resistance; and as they passed along, several of *Mully Ishmael's* People ran to them: *Mully Ishmael's* Coydes, or Governours, acquainted him that the *Algerines* were coming against him: *Mully Ishmael* hearing thereof, raised an Army of Eighty thousand Horse and Foot, and made his Son *Mully Sedan* General thereof.

Whilst his Army was preparing, the *Algerines* were got as far as a Town called *Tezzo*, within two days Journey of *Fez*, where they pitch'd. *Mully Sedan* went against them; and being there, the *Algerines* wrote a Letter to *Mully Ishmael*, acquainting him, that they did not come to fight with his Son, but to have met himself in Person: he sent them word back that his Son was able enough for them.

Soon after they had received his Letter, they engaged *Mully Sedan*'s Army, and slew abundance of them. Many of *Mully Sedan*'s People deserted him, joining with the *Algerines*. Then he sent with all speed to the Emperor his Father, giving him account what had happened.

When *Mully Ishmael* understood that, he gave out, that if any Christians would help, and stand by the great Guns, if he prevailed against the *Algerines*, he would give them their Liberty. So eight *Englishmen* told him they knew what belonged to the Guns, and they would go with him.

So he ordered an hundred *Moors* to assist them, and to take out six great Guns (that they judged might be most serviceable) from the place where they lay betwixt the Walls. They told him they wanted Carriages: He sent for Carpenters immediately, charging them to make Carriages strong and good, and that with all speed, upon pain of losing their Heads in case they neglected.

Mully Sedan again sent the Emperor his Father word, that if he did not hasten to Battel, the *Algerines* would be in *Fez* in four days time. *Mully Ishmael* hearing that, was forced to go with all speed, raising what Forces he could, leaving for haste his Field-pieces behind him.

The Emperor being come where his own Army lay, he made Peace with the *Algerines* General, and in order thereto, gave forty eighty Mules laden with Gold, and an Horse and Furniture worth 200000 Crowns.

Chapter Eleven: The Tyrant's Sheepkeeper

bout a Month before I came from *Macqueness*, one of our own Nation, namely *Elias Roberts*, being by the said Emperor put to look after a parcel of Sheep, he came himself to view them; and telling them over, found three of his number wanting, who thereupon sent for one of his chief Negroes that kept an account of them, and examined him what was become of them?

He replied, the Christian kept the Key, and lock'd them up every Night, and carried it with him to the place where he went to sleep under Ground.

The Tyrant immediately sent his Blood-hounded Negroes to fetch the poor Christian, who was not far from them; being come, he asked him what was become of those Sheep that were wanting? he made Answer, he went home every Night, having first fastned the Door, and that the Negro had a false Key to the Door; so turning to the Negro, and upon Examination finding him faulty, he presently shot him to Death, running his Launce through his Body in several places, and threatned the Christian for not acquainting him therewith sooner, saying, if he would not turn *Moor*, he would kill him, as he had done the *Negro*, who lay dead before them.

The Christian boldly replied, he was brought up in the Faith of Jesus Christ, and he would not turn *Moor*, and that he feared God, whose Power was greater than his; so the Emperor fell to cutting him, and afterwards had him very inhumanly stretched out by those bloody Negroes, and beaten till he was left for dead.

Then he went away to his Works where English Captives were, and told them he had killed one of the Dogs their Brother, for taking no better care of his Sheep, and calling them Dogs in his own Language, and bidding them fetch that Dog away; five or six of them went and brought the poor Man away, who had been so cruelly beaten by the wicked Wretch, his Body was so exceedingly bruised, he could not stir neither hand nor foot; neither could he feed himself for several days, but as we help'd him.

Yet through God's Mercy, he was pretty well recovered before my Departure from thence. And thus when the poor Captives are by this unmerciful, and rather, as we may term him, inhuman Brute, beaten and killed at his pleasure, none dare make any Complaint to him; for instead of taking any Pity of them, he matters no more to kill a Christian than to kill a Dog; and if any of them seeks for Favour from this Tyrant, he's either killed, or sorely beaten by either him or his bloody Negroes.

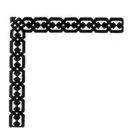

Chapter Twelve: The Escape

A Moor, one of the Natives of the Country, having Compassion on me, and seeing my sad Condition that I was kept daily in, which I cannot at large insert here, came to me, speaking his own Language, being Arabick, knowing I could understand him; and he asked me if I would go to my Native Country?

I replied, Are you in earnest or not? he answered, Yes, and would direct me, and go along with me himself to *Marsegan*, a Garison belonging to the King of *Portugal*.

I told him, if he expected any Reward or Satisfaction from me for his Pains, I had nothing to give him; he said he knew that by my Condition. So I enquired of him where he lived? he answered, at a place called *Assimore*, which is not far from the Christian Garison; and he said, he would trust to the Benevolence of the Governour of that place, provided I would speak to the said Governour for a Gratuity for him, when we should arrive there: I told him I should be worse than a Jew, if I did not do that; and they themselves count the Jews the worst and falsest of all People.

Then I asked him in what time we should provide for our Journey? he said, as soon as I could find convenient opportunity; and I farther prevailed with him to take in two more English-men along with us, whose Names were *Tristram Bryan*, born in *Plymouth*, and *Edward Tucker*, who came from *New-England*.

And in five days time after we were fitted with a small quantity of Bread for the Journey, supposing we might accomplish our Journey in ten Nights time, for we must of necessity hide our selves in the Day for fear of being discovered; yet we found it difficult enough to perform in two and twenty days, in which time we were put to great Hardships and Necessities on the way. The Particulars are as follow.

On the 26th of *June*, 1692, in the Evening, we set forward from *Macqueness*, and travelled as far as we could that Night in great fear of being pursued, with our *Moor* to direct us in the way, knowing that if they had found us, we had been killed, if not burnt, which would have been the *Moor*'s Lot had we been taken: towards day we had a great River to pass; when we were got over, we found a small Coppise or Wood, where we rested the Day following, being the 27th.

In the Evening when the Sun was set, our Guide was forward to be going, not knowing how the Event would prove, and I had much ado to perswade him from going before 'twas dark.

When we came into the Road out of the Wood we met ten *Moors*, and Mules and Asses laden with Goods for the Emperor, being Iron, which they had taken from one *Savage* an English Master that came from *Bilboa*; so we followed our Guide the *Moor*, who gave them the time of the Night, and they him likewise; and so we passed that time without any further trouble, they supposing us to be *Moors*, being we had on their sort of Apparel.

So we travelled that Night, making what haste we could, and still in great fear, lest we should have been discovered by the *Moors*: when we rested, it was towards Day, in some Brambles or Bushes, seeing them pass along by us, driving of Sheep and Bullocks; but through Mercy they did not see us.

And the next Night, being the 28th, we travelled all Night; and when Day appeared, we could not find a convenient place to lodg in, which we sought for; and about Sun-rising we found a place betwixt two Mountains where were Holes made with the Winter Rains coming off the Hills near a Path-way, to which we made, and espied several *Moors* who went along the Road, that had Mules and Asses loaden with Iron, who saw us not.

Some part of the Day we slept; and the *Moor* and I watcht; in which time the *Moor* gathered Palm, and made a Sling, to sling Stones at Lions and other wild Beasts that appeared.

So in the Evening, after Sunset, (being the 29th) we travelled till we came to a River-side, where were a great parcel of *Moors* and *Mules* a baiting, that had Bail-Goods, which the *Sally-*

Moors had taken in Prizes, to carry to the Emperor at *Macqueness*; who strictly enquired of our *Moor*, from whence we came, and whither we were going?

He made answer, To *Salley*, and came from *Macqueness*, and so our *Moor* bad them Good-night; and we travelled on(without further enquiry) along the River-side before we could get over.

When we were over, there were a great many Bramble-bushes and Rush-bushes; and our *Moor* feared there were Lions in that Place, so we made what haste we could up a Hill, on the top of which was a great Plain; and being very thirsty, we travelled on a good way further, and heard a noise of Frogs and Toads; to which Place we came, and found a standing Water, which stunk; however we drank thereof to stay our Thirst, and ⟨twas sweet to us: and so went on till we found a ruined Castle, which had formerly belonged to the *Portugues*, at which our *Moor* would fain have rested; but I told him there might happen to be *Moors* there, because they usually rested in such Places in the Night.

So we went further, till we came to a place where grew a great parcel of high Weeds, and there we rested that Day.

The 30th at Night, after Sunset, we set forwards; but were very thirsty, the Sun having shone hot upon us that Day, having lain without shelter, only the Weeds.

I asked our *Moor*, how long it would be e're we could find any Water? He said, A little further there was a small River; but we thought it a long way to it, our Throats being so parch'd with Drought; so we drank Water, and eat a little Bread, which did greatly refresh us; and we went forward till near break of Day, where we rested in some Weeds till about two in the Afternoon; at which time three Women disturbed us two or three times, but saw not our Faces: So we three went forward, and our *Moor* stood, and enquired of them the way to *Salley*.

Then the Women asked from whence we came? Who answered, From *Tapholet*, which was a City in that Country. They further asked, if he had lain in that place all Night? and asked what they were that were with him? He told them, Three of his Neighbours, and that they had lain there all Night, being Strangers.

They said, It was a wonder that the Lions had not destroyed us, there being so many in that place, they devoured some of their

Cattel almost every Night; and they told him it was about four Leagues to *Salley*.

After Sunset (*July* 1.) we travelled till we came to a Wood, where the *Moor* would have had us to rest; but seeing of Lights which the Country People had in their Tents, and hearing a Lion roar thereabouts, we went further, and came to a ruined Tower, where was a good Spring of Water; we drank and refreshed our selves, but durst not stay for fear of *Moors* being in that place; and going a little farther, we came into a Valley, where was a Hole the Winter Rains had made, there we rested; and after the Sun was risen, two *Moors* came to cut Palm: At which I awaked our *Moor*, who spoke to them, and gave them the time of Day, and they likewise to him.

They enquired of him from whence he came, and whither he was going? He told them, he came from beyond *Tapholet*, and was going to visit a great Saint at a Town called *Temsnah*; and asked further, if there were none with him? He answered, there were three more. They asked, if we had lain there all Night?

He said, we had; They said, it was to be wondred that the Lions had not devoured us; and came to look at us where we lay, speaking *Arabick*; but the *Moor* told them, we could not speak that *Lingua*; and we were covered all over with our white Blankets, being such as the *Moors* commonly wear. So they went away and left us, telling us, We did well in going to visit the Saint.

So we got up, and espying a parcel of Bushes a little distance off, we removed thither, lest the two *Moors* should have informed of us at *Salley*, and so have come back to the place and found us.

The Bush where we were hid, was near a River-side, but we durst not go to drink thereat, by reason of People which passed to and fro there by us all Day long.

July 2. After Sun-Set, we attempted to go over the River; but it being so strong a Stream, and deep, we could not pass over it: And in our going a great way further up the River-side, there happened to be several of the *Moors*; yet being Night, they saw us not, save only one Man of the Natives, which had tied up a bundle of Canes fast together to pass over the River with them; to whom our *Moor* gave the time of the Night; and he answering with the like to us, we parted: and going higher up, we found a place not so deep as the other part of the River; so got over, and travelled up a Hill on the other side, where we found some Bushes, and there we rested, and our *Moor* lay on the out-side of them.

In the Morning when the Sun was risen, came by us two *Moors* with two Asses, who said one to the other, it was wonder the Lions had not devoured that Man, meaning our *Moor*, who they saw lying by the side of the Bushes.

On the third Instant, after the Sun was set, we set forward, endeavouring to get to the Sea-side: but there being several People in the way, watching with their Dogs to keep the wild Beasts from their Gardens; which we hearing, were fain to flee further from them: so we travelled a little further, and rested among some Rushes.

The next Night, being the 4th of *July*, we travelled after Sun-setting as far as we could, being weary and faint, and rested.

On the 5th; on which Day after Sun was set, we set forward, and travelled till we came to a place where was a standing Water, being thereto led by a noise of Frogs; which although the Water stunk, yet drinking thereof, it was sweet to us; with that, and a little Bread, we were much refreshed; but at this time our Bread was gone, so we travelled a little further, and rested.

The 6th Instant, after Sunset, we went forward, and discovered a great many Lights which the Natives had in their Tents where they lodg: So we parted a while one from another, to find out the Roads.

At length I came to a place where the Country People use to go to Market, where we again met together; and travelling awhile, we heard some Dogs, as I thought, did scent us; and near that place we met with a Lion lying by the Way-side; which the *Moor* seeing, before he roused, he struck him fair over the Head.

So the Lion roared at him, and followed us half a Mile or more; but our *Moor* kept slinging of Stones at him so fast, that he left us. Then we came to a Valley, where was a Wood on each side: When Day appeared, we rested in the Wood, having no Bread to sustain us; but we durst not enter the Wood till it was Daylight, for fear of the Lions: We then found a piece of Pot in the Wood, with which our *Moor* brought us some Water out of the Valley; for we durst not fetch it our selves, lest the People saw us: so when the *Moor* had brought us a Pot full of Water, (but in the mean time we were lamenting our sad Condition for want of Bread, having then no Sustenance but Palm-Berries, Grass and Weeds, and any thing we could eat, which was sweet to us) he said, in his own Language, God was great. So went from us about the space of four Hours; in which time he sold his Sash, and bought us a small quantity of Bread (about a pound and an half) therewith, and brought us a little of it, which we ate; and he fetch'd us a little more Water in the Pot: After we had eaten and drank of the Water, we went to sleep, two us watching.

On the 7th, after Sun-set, we travelled on; and the *Moor* slung Stones, whilst we passed through the Wood, lest there be Lions lurking thereabouts: having refreshed our selves with the Bread and Water, we rested amongst some Brambles, but could find no more Water that Night.

Then on the 8th Day at Night we came to another Wood, in which we travelled a great way, and kept two of us awake to watch against Lions and other wild Beasts.

On the 9th we set forward, and travelled in the same Wood, and still had no Water.

The 10th, after Sun-setting, we went till we came to an Hill of Rocks; at the bottom whereof we found a Spring of Water, and drinking thereof, we were greatly refreshed: and there was a little River, from which we went, till we came to some Trees or Bushes, and there rested.

About eight a Clock in the Morning, *July* 11. (it raining fast) we ventured to travel that Day, after we had rubb'd out a little Corn, and eaten, that the *Moor* had brought us, having no Bread to eat: so went to the top of an Hill, on which grew a Tree, which we climb'd upon, and espied the Sea at a great distance from us.

We travelled all that Day, and the Night following, till towards Day, that we rested, but had neither Bread nor Water.

On the 12th at Night, after Sun-setting, we travelled a good way, and heard a noise of Frogs and Toads; to which we made, and found Water, which we drank of; and although it was very brackish, yet it was pleasant to us, by reason of our sore Drought.

A little from thence we met with a Person of Quality, as we judged by his Habit and Attendance, having ten Men with him; to whom our *Moor* paid his Respects, and gave him the time of the Night. He answered him again in his own Language, and asked him whither we were going? Our *Moor* answered, To *Santa Cruse*: So he bid us, God speed: Afterwards our *Moor* asked him from whence he came? He answered, From *Assimore*. So we departed away, and travelled till we found some Bushes, wherein we rested that Day.

July 13. After Sun-setting we set out, and came so near *Assimore*, that, listening, we heard the People in it, and saw the Town, which stood on the South-side of a Hill, and a River by the Town, which was so deep, that we could not get over, because one of our Men could not swim.

Then we travelled along the North-side of the River, till we came to a place here Cains grew, and there we rested by the River-side.

July 14. After it was Day, our *Moor* went to see his Family which dwelt there in that Town. We having been a considerable time without Bread, I requested our *Moor* to bring us a little, (which he did) and likewise to see if he could find any thing to carry my Country-man over the River; and about four in the Afternoon he returned with some Bread, and said, he had found a Tree.

After Sun was set, we went to view it, and found it not fit to swim withal: So we returned, and went back to the Cains, and there staid. On the 15th Instant, when the Sun was risen, I desired our *Moor* to go and enquire of the People, where we might pass over the River? The People told him, there was no Passage but by a Boat at the Town. So our *Moor* went about a League further in the Country, where he saw a Man and a Woman upon a Mule crossing the River, and marked the place with some Stones, that we might find it, and so returned to us, and rested till Sun-setting.

So we set forward, and had gone but a little way before we heard a Lion roar, but he did not come in our sight; then we came to the place where the *Moor* laid his Mark, and sat down to consult how to pass over there, we hearing of People in a Garden were near at hand: and in the interim, we heard a Lion just behind us; so we hastened and got over the River, and travelled a little further, and rested.

July 16. After Sun-setting we travelled about a Mile further, where we saw a Town, that our *Moor* said was a Saint's Town, to which the People, that were not able to pay their Taxes to the Emperor, fled for Refuge.

July 17. After Sun-setting we travelled; and going till about Midnight we came within call of the Garison,[2] which was at *Mersygan*, belonging to the King of *Portugal*: So I called out, and the Souldiers made answer to me, and asked what we were? I replied, We were three Christians and a *Moor*: Which they presently acquainted the Governour of, and bid us hasten nearer, lest there should be any *Moors* in the hearing of us. Which we did, and running to a wrong place, they called to us again to make to the two Draw-bridges, where we sate down.

So the Governour, and the rest of the Officers, came to the Wall; and after he had examined us, he and the Guard let us in; and he ordered his Servants to bring us into the House, and to give us some Relief; and he himself came to us, and wondred that so little satisfied us in our eating and drinking: So had us into another Room, and asked me, If I did not know of three Men that were taken by the *Moors* from that Garison?

I answered, I knew of two, but not of the third. He bid me speak to the *Moor*, and ask him, If he would undertake to bring them thither to that place? So I spoke to the *Moor*, who bid me tell the Governour, That he would endeavour it to the utmost of his Power.

So the Governour ordered us a Lodging; and in the Morning ordered his Clerk to write a couple of Letters, and gave them to the *Moor*, with forty pieces of Eight for bringing us thither, saying, If he did bring the two Portugueses, he would give him as much more as should maintain his Family as long as he lived.

The *Moor* said, He would do his endeavour. So the Governour ordered Dinner for us: And about four a Clock he again sent for me and the *Moor*; and bid me tell him, in his Language, That if he feared any thing in his Return, he would send some of his Troopers to conduct him on the Way.

The *Moor* made answer, He should go more safe alone. After Sun was set, the Governour gave him Victuals to serve him, till he could shift for himself. And the *Moor* taking his leave, returned, and went on his Journey.

About three Weeks after, a Portuguese Man of War came into that Garison to fetch about 1800 Souldiers off from thence: So I

---

[2] The distance between *Macqueness* and *Marsegan*, being two hundred Miles or more; but travelling in the Night, occasioned our missing the Way: so that we went at least three hundred Miles before we came to the Garison.

desired of the Governour we might go aboard with them: Which he was willing, and in four Days after we had been aboard, most of the Souldiers being come off, the Captain sent a Letter to the Governour, by the Coxon of the Pinnace, desiring him to hasten the remainder away.

When the Pinnace went ashore, his Crew wondered to see any *Moors* there, and asked, What they did there? The Portuges told them, They came with a Flag of Truce, to treat for three *Moors* they had taken. They offered the Governour two thousand Dollars for them, being one of them was a Shack, or Governour; or Bullocks, or Sheep, or Corn, in lieu of Money.

He answered, No; for they had taken three Troopers belonging to his Garison; and he heard that two of them were at *Macqueness*. They replied, They knew by whom he heard that, for the *Christians* that the *Moor* brought, had acquainted him therewith; but he had paid dearly for it, for, said they, he was taken with the Pieces of Eight, and Letters about him, and carried up to the Emperor and burnt: At which the Governour was very sorry when he heard it.

The Governour then told them, he heard two of his Troopers were alive at *Macqueness*, but he feared the third was dead, because he heard nothing of him; and bid them go up to the Emperor, and prevail with him, if they could, for the two *Christians*, and bring them, and they should have the three *Moors*.

They told him, they could not do that. He made answer, Then they should never have the *Moors*. So at Night when they came on Board, I asked them what was the best News? Who said, Very bad; for they had seen a parcel of *Moors*, who had given account to the Governour, that the *Moor* that brought us to the Garison, was taken and burnt. At which I was much grieved, knowing the poor *Moor*'s true-heartedness towards us, in bringing and directing us on our Journey, when we made our escape from *Macqueness*.

So setting sail for *Lisbon*, through God's Mercy we safely arrived there, and went to the King's Palace, giving him Thanks for the Kindness the Governour had bestowed upon us, and the *Moor* that brought us to the Garison.

When we came thither, several of the Nobility enquired of us, What Nation we were of? and told us, if we desired it, we might speak with the King; and acquainted him of us, who ordered us to come before him; and enquired of us if we could speak French or Portuguese?

I said we could speak some *Portuguese*, and a little *Lingua Franc*: So he enquired from whence we came? And I gave him account of our narrow escape from that Slavery we had been in under the Emperor, &c. and told him how our Bread was gone in ten Days time, and that we had been two and twenty Days in coming from *Macqueness* to the Garison, and did eat nothing but Reach till the 23d Night.

He much wondered how we were kept alive the rest of the time after our Bread was gone. I told him, through God's Assistance we had shifted as well as we could; for our Liberty being sweet to us, had caused us to run these great hazards we were exposed to.

He further enquired after those *Christians* that are still in Slavery; of which I gave him an Account of all I could remember: And desired him, out of the abundance of his Goodness and Clemency to remember them in their Afflictions. He told me, it was more than he ever heard before, and said, he would, before Winter came, take care to send them Relief, to buy them Victuals and Clothes; and enquired of me, Whether any of his Subjects desired me to lay their Condition before him?

I answered, No; but (by God's Permission) I had in part undergone the same Afflictions they were in, and knew well enough how it was with them. He made answer, God would bless me for it. He likewise asked, If I knew what number of Ships were at *Salley*? I told him, eleven Sail. He said, He knew *Venetia*, for he had formerly been at his Palace.

I said, It was our late King *James*'s Pleasure to give him his Liberty; with much more that passed betwixt us.

When this *Venetia* returned home to the Emperor, the Emperor ordered him to build a Ship; and several English-men, that were newly taken Slaves he caused to draw Timber in a Cart from *Memora* to *Salley* (which was twelve Miles distant) like so many Oxen, driving and whipping of them in a very barbarous manner.

The Name of *Venetia* caused me to insert this here, to show the barbarous Cruelty of this inhumane Wretch; and so I shall leave him, and proceed. We having taken our leaves here, took our Passage for *Holland*, where my two Country-men staid; but I took my passage for *England*, where, praised be God for his Great Mercies, I arrived safely, being by his good Providence at last delivered from under the Hands of this Inhumane Tyrant, and his Hellish Crew of Negroes; beseeching Almighty God, that all my Country-men, in all their Affairs and Negotiations, may ever escape from his cruel Hands.

Francis Brooks.
FINIS.

CPSIA information can be obtained
at www.ICGtesting.com
Printed in the USA
BVHW042024141020
591015BV00010B/106